THE OFFICIAL ENGLAND
WORLD CUP GUIDE 2002

Gerry Cox with Mark Knowles

Contents

Chapter 1

England's Route to the Finals	4
Sven-Göran Eriksson Profile	6
England Player Profiles	8

Chapter 2

Introduction to the World Cup Finals	20
The Venues	22
The Stadia	24
Tournament Rules, Golden Boot Award, FIFA Fair Play Awards	26

Chapter 3

Meet the Teams	28
World Superstars	46
Players to Watch out for	52

Chapter 4

World Cup Trivia, Facts and Stats	54
World Cup Quiz	56
Quiz/Crossword Answers	58
World Cup Crossword	59
World Cup Progress Chart	**60**

CARLTON BOOKS

England's Route to the World Cup Finals

England's efforts to qualify for the World Cup finals were nothing less than heroic. After Kevin Keegan resigned following the opening defeat by Germany, Sven-Göran Eriksson's side battled from bottom of Group 9 to the top and through to South Korea and Japan. These are the highlights of their dramatic journey.

07.10.2000, Wembley: England 0–1 Germany

Liverpool midfielder Dietmar Hamann scores the game's only goal as Germany take all three points at Wembley Stadium – prompting Kevin Keegan to resign. Not a great start!

24.03.2001, Anfield: England 2–1 Finland

England, now under new manager Sven-Göran Eriksson, trail to Finland before goals from Anfield hero Michael Owen (pictured left) and David Beckham clinch a crucial victory.

06.06.2001, Athens: Greece 0–2 England

Scholes scores again and new skipper David Beckham curls in a free-kick to give Eriksson his fifth consecutive victory (including friendlies).

05.09.2001, St James' Park: England 2–0 Albania

Michael Owen and Robbie Fowler score in another dominant performance. England are just one game from qualification.

GROUP 9 FINAL TABLE

	Pld	W	D	L	F	A	GD	Pts
ENGLAND	8	5	2	1	16	6	10	17
Germany	8	5	2	1	14	10	4	17
Finland	8	3	3	2	12	7	5	12
Greece	8	2	1	5	7	17	-10	7
Albania	8	1	0	7	5	14	-9	3

11.10.2000, Helsinki: Finland 0-0 England

Four days later, technical director Howard Wilkinson oversees a tricky stalemate. In the following weeks The Football Association considers the candidates for the position of permanent England manager.

28.03.2001, Tirana: Albania 1-3 England

Andy Cole slots in his first international goal, with Paul Scholes and Michael Owen also on the scoresheet to clinch England's first away win of the World Cup qualifying campaign.

01.09.2001, Munich: Germany 1-5 England

The result that stunned the world. Owen's hat-trick and goals from Steven Gerrard and Emile Heskey complete the most famous victory over Germany since 1966.

06.10.2001, Old Trafford: England 2-2 Greece

Greece strike first before substitute Teddy Sheringham scores with his first touch. Greece score again, but with time running out Beckham scores another beauty with a sublime free-kick – England are through!

Profile: Sven-Göran Eriksson

When Sven-Göran Eriksson was appointed national coach at the end of October 2000 he made history by becoming the first foreigner ever to manage England.

It was a brave appointment by The Football Association, and one which was criticised by many. But Eriksson, who was a successful club manager at Lazio, Sampdoria, Benfica, Fiorentina, Roma and Gothenburg answered his critics in remarkable style – by guiding England to the World Cup finals in a manner which not even their most ardent fan could have dreamed of.

England were bottom of World Cup qualifying Group 9 when the Swede took over, with many fans believing it was going to be very difficult to qualify from second place via the play-offs and almost impossible to qualify automatically.

But once Eriksson had become the first England manager ever to win his first five games in charge, things changed dramatically. And by the time England beat Germany 5–1 in Munich, the transformation from also-rans to group winners was all but complete, assuming there would be no slip-ups against Albania and Greece.

So what is his secret?

Well, Eriksson, who had an ordinary playing career in Scandinavia, is a man who leaves absolutely

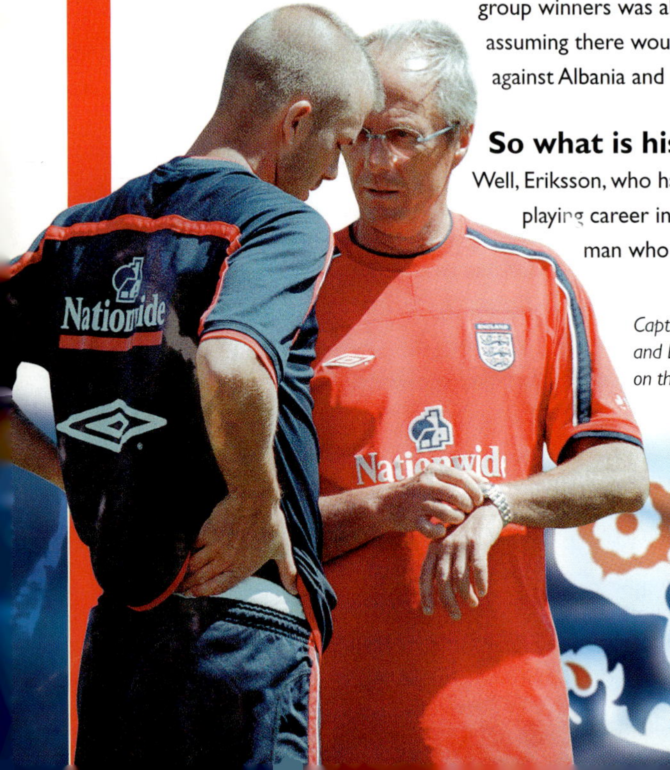

Captain David Beckham and Eriksson discuss tactics on the training ground

nothing to chance. His preparation is faultless and he has become famous for attending as many matches as he can fit into his working week.

But aside from that, his footballing philosophies are simple. He plays players in positions they are used to, in a formation they understand and with instructions that are clear. And he organises it all with a natural air of authority and calm which has united the England camp in respect for him.

Together with his trusty assistant Tord Grip he will use all the psychological motivation and every management tool he can to fill his squad with confidence.

SVEN-GÖRAN ERIKSSON: CAREER DETAILS

1948:	Born February 5th in Torsby, Sweden
1966–75:	Defender for Karlskogen (Swedish 2nd Division)
1979–82:	Manager of IFK Gothenburg, wins UEFA Cup
1982–84:	Benfica: wins two league titles, one cup
1984–87:	AS Roma: wins Italian Cup
1987–89:	Fiorentina
1989–92:	Benfica: wins league title
1992–97:	Sampdoria: wins Italian Cup
1997–2000:	Lazio: wins Cup-Winners' Cup, league title 2000
2000:	October 31, becomes England's first foreign coach

David Beckham

If England are to pose any serious claim to winning the 2002 World Cup trophy, then much will depend on captain David Beckham.

The Manchester United star has become the key man for Sven-Göran Eriksson and was extremely impressive throughout the qualifying campaign.

There was good reasoning in handing Beckham the captain's armband – he can do everything: shoot, pass, tackle and he covers the whole pitch in doing so.

Fans will be hoping to see more of his trademark free-kicks in the tournament, although none could better his last-second effort against Greece, which assured England's place in Japan and South Korea.

Beckham is the leader of his side and has won the nation's respect for bouncing back from the lowest point in his career, when he was sent off against Argentina at the last World Cup.

Expect to see a determined Beckham, keen to show he has learned from the mistake of four years ago and to cement his place as one of the world's greatest players.

FACT FILE

Club: Manchester United
Date of Birth: 02.05.1975
Position: Midfielder
England debut: 1996 v Moldova
Tournaments: WC 1998, EC 2000

Steven Gerrard

When England played in the last World Cup in France in 1998, Steven Gerrard had not even made his debut for his club side Liverpool.

Four years later and the talented midfielder should be one of the first names on the team-sheet following an amazing rise to the top.

Gerrard will only just have turned 22 by the time the competition in Japan and South Korea begins, but his strength, tenacious tackling, precision passing and powerful shooting make him one of England's key players.

The youngster made his international debut shortly before the European Championship in 2000, but made only one appearance as a substitute against Germany in that competition.

Since then he has become one of the most complete midfielders in the Premiership, driving Liverpool to the Worthington Cup, FA Cup and UEFA Cup treble in 2001.

And he smashed a brilliant goal, the first for his country, in the 5–1 thrashing of Germany that put England well on their way to qualifying for this World Cup.

FACT FILE

Club: Liverpool
Date of Birth: 30.05.1980
Position: Midfielder
England debut: 2000 v Ukraine
Tournaments: EC 2000

Paul Scholes

The quiet but lethal 27-year-old Manchester United star has earned himself a reputation as one of the world's best goalscoring midfielders.

Not only does Paul Scholes possess an incredible record of scoring one goal every three games for England, but he also has the knack of scoring in important fixtures for his country.

So far in his international career Scholes has scored goals in the World Cup finals in France, in a crucial Euro 2000 play-off match against Scotland in Glasgow, and in the 2000 European Championship finals themselves in Holland and Belgium.

And the great thing about Paul Scholes, who was named the England Team Player of the Year in 2000, is that he can score from just about anywhere on the football pitch. Long-range efforts, spectacular volleys, cool tap-ins and clever flicks are all in his repertoire.

It's not just about goals either. His club boss Sir Alex Ferguson once described him as the best passer of the ball at Old Trafford.

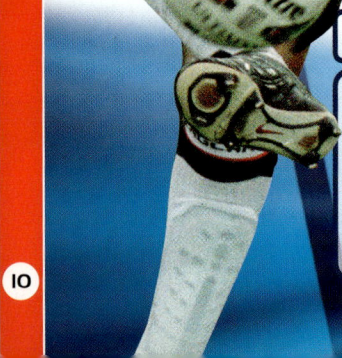

FACT FILE

Club: Manchester United
Date of Birth: 16.11.1974
Position: Midfielder
England debut: 1997 v Italy
Tournaments: WC 1998, EC 2000

Rio Ferdinand

Rio Ferdinand is no stranger to handling the big pressure, having become the world's most expensive defender when he left West Ham to join Leeds for £18 million in November 2000.

Already described as "the next Bobby Moore", Ferdinand has shown no problems coping with the massive fee resting on his shoulders and has only got better working under manager David O'Leary at Elland Road.

Ferdinand is composed on the ball as well as being a strong and mobile defender. He can play his way out of most situations and can be relied upon to get his side out of danger.

He won his first cap under Sven-Göran Eriksson in February 2001 in a 3–0 friendly win over Spain and has formed an impressive partnership with Sol Campbell at the heart of the England defence.

Ferdinand will be hoping to make up for the disappointment of missing out on the Euro 2000 Championship and to show his ability on the world stage this summer.

FACT FILE

Club: Leeds United
Date of Birth: 07.11.1978
Position: Defender
England debut: 1997 v Cameroon
Tournaments: None

Michael Owen

Owen, scorer of that wonder goal against Argentina in the 1998 World Cup, is a national hero once again after his stunning hat-trick in the 5–1 demolition of Germany during qualification.

He made his debut for Liverpool at 17 and burst into the England team just 12 months later, becoming the youngest England international of the century. From 1997 to 1999, he established himself as Liverpool's top goalscorer, with 18 goals in both seasons, before a hamstring injury interrupted his staggering progress in April 2000.

The star player for the England team in France '98, his second-round goal against Argentina, a brilliant solo effort, is considered to be one of the World Cup's greatest.

Michael Owen's major strength is his ball control at pace – he can run 100 metres in comfortably under 11 seconds. Though he is already one of football's best-known strikers, an injury-free World Cup will guarantee that this life-long fan of Liverpool will appear on the wanted lists of many clubs.

FACT FILE

Club: Liverpool
Date of Birth: 14.12.1979
Position: Striker
England debut: 1998 v Chile
Tournaments: WC 1998, EC 2000

Teddy Sheringham

Even in his mid-30s, Teddy Sheringham is still one of England's leading players, able to link midfield and attack by playing in behind his fellow striker and also to win and hold up the ball.

The Spurs striker has had a glittering career that has seen him win medals at domestic and European level, as well as appearing in the World Cup and European Championship.

Sheringham has always been able to think more quickly than his marker and create as well as finish goalscoring chances with his head and both feet.

At the age of 35, during his final season with Manchester United, he was voted Footballer of the Year by both fellow players and journalists. He had helped United win the 1999 European Cup when he scored one late goal and set up another to beat Bayern Munich.

He started his career with Millwall, before big money moves to Nottingham Forest, Spurs and Manchester United. Now back at Tottenham, he is still a formidable force for both club and country.

FACT FILE

Club: Tottenham Hotspur
Date of Birth: 02.04.1966
Position: Striker
England debut: 1993 v Poland
Tournaments: EC 1996, WC 1998, EC 2000

Sol Campbell

Having decided to make the move from Tottenham to fierce London rivals Arsenal last summer, the World Cup should hold no fears for Sol Campbell.

Campbell has become a leading figure at the heart of the English defence since making his debut against Hungary in 1996 and has benefited from playing in the Champions League for Arsenal. Strong in the tackle and in the air, and with a powerful physique, Campbell's defensive partnership with Rio Ferdinand could lay down the foundation of England's campaign.

FACT FILE

Club: Arsenal
Date of Birth: 18.09.1974
Position: Defender
England debut: 1996 v Hungary
Tournaments: EC 1996, WC 1998, EC 2000

Gary Neville

The older brother of club and country team-mate Phil, Gary Neville has been the unsung hero of the England defence for many years now. His partnership with close friend David Beckham down the right is a crucial part of the England gameplan and he rarely lets his club or country down, having won countless honours with Manchester United. The right-back has had few challengers for his position in recent times, but it is still a major achievement to chalk up 50 international caps by your 27th birthday – a feat he looks certain to achieve.

FACT FILE

Club: Manchester United
Date of Birth: 18.02.1975
Position: Defender
England debut: 1995 v Japan
Tournaments: EC 1996, WC 1998, EC 2000

David Seaman

The Arsenal goalkeeper is hoping to live up to his nickname of "Safe Hands" in this summer's finals – as long as he gets over his recent injury problems.

Seaman is no stranger to big tournaments, having played in France '98 and in two European Championships, as well as winning a host of medals with Arsenal. Despite approaching 40, his experience at national and club level means he is still one of the top goalkeepers in the Premiership and can always be relied on.

FACT FILE

Club: Arsenal
Date of Birth: 19.09.1963
Position: Goalkeeper
England debut: 1988 v Saudi Arabia
Tournaments: EC 1996, WC 1998, EC 2000

Andy Cole

The experienced striker is the highest-scoring Englishman in European club football, but has struggled to translate that form to international level. Cole made his name at Newcastle before a £7 million move to Manchester United, where he won countless honours. But after finding himself on the bench too often, he moved to Blackburn Rovers last December for regular first-team action.

FACT FILE

Club: Blackburn Rovers
Born: 15.10.1971
Position: Striker
England debut: 1995 v Uruguay
Tournaments: EC 2000

Martin Keown

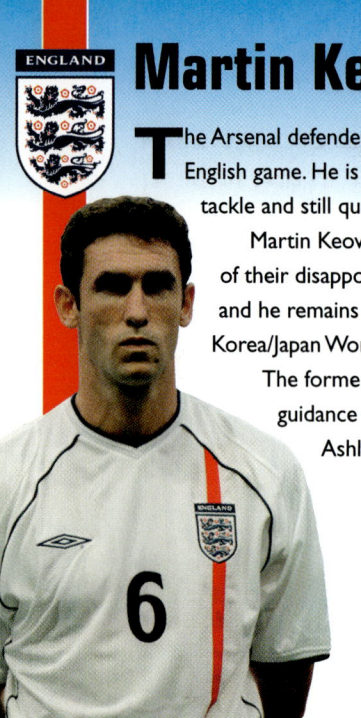

The Arsenal defender is known as one of the best man-markers in the English game. He is experienced, cool under pressure, tough in the tackle and still quick in his mid-30s.

Martin Keown was one of the few England players to come out of their disappointing campaign at Euro 2000 with some praise, and he remains a crucial part of their defensive plans for the Korea/Japan World Cup.

The former Aston Villa and Everton stopper will provide guidance to younger defenders like Rio Ferdinand and Ashley Cole.

FACT FILE

Club: Arsenal
Date of Birth: 24.07.1966
Position: Defender
England debut: 1992 v France
Tournaments: EC 1992, WC 1998, EC 2000

Robbie Fowler

Fowler's £11 million move to Leeds last November followed a period in which he'd struggled to gain regular first-team football at Liverpool, where he was a hero among the club's supporters.

Fowler emerged as a teenage sensation for the Reds in the early 1990s, breaking all sorts of scoring records. But he failed to produce that form for England and a succession of injuries has disrupted his career in recent years. On his day, though, he is the most natural finisher in Britain.

FACT FILE

Club: Leeds United
Date of Birth: 09.04.1975
Position: Striker
England debut: 1996 v Bulgaria
Tournaments: EC 1996, EC 2000

Darren Anderton

The Tottenham Hotspur midfielder is one of the Premiership's most athletic and creative footballers, but his career has been blighted by a succession of injuries.

But it has not stopped him playing in two European Championships and the 1998 World Cup finals, and he was one of England's first-choice players before David Beckham became a regular in midfield.

Genuinely two-footed and a great crosser of the ball, the former Portsmouth player could be the answer to England's prayers on the left of midfield.

FACT FILE

Club: Tottenham Hotspur
Born: 03.03.1972
Position: Midfielder
England debut: 1994 v Denmark
Tournaments: EC 1996, WC 1998, EC 2000

Emile Heskey

Striker Heskey is a nightmare for defenders with his immense physical power and dangerous pace. His performances at Liverpool since his move from Leicester City for £10 million two years ago have brought international caps and his understanding with Owen there has proved valuable for England. Though superb at holding the ball up in the centre, he's also been employed on the wing.

FACT FILE

Club: Liverpool
Date of Birth: 11.01.1978
Position: Striker
England debut: 1999 v Hungary
Tournaments: EC 2000

Ashley Cole

One of the youngest players in the England squad, Ashley Cole has made an impressively rapid rise to the top by filling the troublesome left-back position.

He was called-up for his debut against Albania during the qualifying campaign, despite having only broken into the Arsenal side a few months earlier.

Tenacious tackling and pace taking the ball forward when turning defence into attack are this young player's strong points.

FACT FILE

Club: Arsenal
Date of Birth: 20.12.1980
Position: Defender
England debut: 2001 v Albania
Tournaments: None

Gareth Southgate

Seen as very reliable in the Premiership and a consistent performer at international level, Southgate is both versatile and dependable, which makes him an excellent squad player. He rose to prominence for England during Euro '96, but was remembered for his penalty miss in the semi-final shoot-out against Germany rather than his excellent performances. Southgate started his career as a midfielder with Crystal Palace before becoming a defender with Aston Villa and then moving to Middlesbrough last summer.

FACT FILE

Club: Middlesbrough
Date of birth: 03.09.1970
Position: Defender
England debut: 1995 v Portugal
Tournaments: EC 1996, WC 1998, EC 2000

Nigel Martyn

Martyn was the first £1 million goalkeeper in Britain when he moved from Bristol Rovers to Crystal Palace in 1989, but his career really flourished at Leeds.

He is now a regular in the England squad and made some crucial saves in the final qualifier against Greece.

If David Seaman is fit, Martyn may have to settle for a place on the bench, but Sven-Göran Eriksson knows he has a good back-up ready to step in.

FACT FILE

Club: Leeds United
Date of Birth: 11.08.1966
Position: Goalkeeper
England debut: 1992 v CIS
Tournaments: WC 1998, EC 2000

Other Contenders

One of Sven-Göran Eriksson's toughest tasks has been to choose the final squad of 22 to take to the Far East, and at the time of this book going to press, nothing was finalised. But front-runners among the contenders for other places in the final England squad were goalkeepers Richard Wright (Arsenal) and David James (West Ham), utility players such as Phil Neville (Man Utd) and Jamie Carragher (Liverpool) and rising defenders Wes Brown (Man Utd) and Ledley King (Tottenham). Midfielders in the reckoning included Steve McManaman (Real Madrid), Kieron Dyer (Newcastle), Nick Barmby (Liverpool) and Joe Cole (West Ham), and up front Kevin Phillips (Sunderland) and Alan Smith (Leeds) were pressing for a place.

Introduction to the World Cup and to hosts South Korea and Japan

The World Cup, played every four years, is the most popular sporting spectacle on Earth, even surpassing the Olympic Games and other major football tournaments.

Below: The World Cup finals are in Asia for the first time
Bottom: The French team celebrate their home victory in the 1998 World Cup

The statistics are staggering: 15,000 participants (players, staff, organisers, media, etc.) for 64 games between 32 countries during a month, a total audience in 196 countries of 41 billion watching 30,000 hours of televised football, with the final watched by around 1 billion viewers – one sixth of the planet's population. Many less watch the games live, with total attendances at France '98 reaching around 2.5 million.

The finals are held in a different continent each time and this year's tournament will be co-hosted by South Korea and Japan, the first time two countries have shared duties. Both countries are relatively new to football, and indeed Japan only introduced a professional league ten years ago.

The final 32 teams have been whittled down through a qualifying tournament lasting almost two years, with 194 countries playing 777 games.

South Korea and Japan qualify automatically as hosts, along with the reigning champions France, and the rest of the finalists are made up of regional group winners and those who made it through the play-off system.

They will all gather for football's ultimate test, which began in 1930 and was interrupted only by the Second World War. Only seven countries have ever won the tournament, with Brazil the most successful as four-times winners. Who will it be this time?

WORLD CUP WINNERS

Year	Winners	Runners-up	Venue
1930	Uruguay	Argentina	Uruguay
1934	Italy	Czechoslovakia	Italy
1938	Italy	Hungary	France
1950	Uruguay	Brazil	Brazil
1954	W Germany	Hungary	Switzerland
1958	Brazil	Sweden	Sweden
1962	Brazil	Czechoslovakia	Chile
1966	England	W Germany	England
1970	Brazil	Italy	Mexico
1974	W Germany	Holland	W Germany
1978	Argentina	Holland	Argentina
1982	Italy	W Germany	Spain
1986	Argentina	W Germany	Mexico
1990	W Germany	Argentina	Italy
1994	Brazil	Italy	USA
1998	France	Brazil	France

The Venues

There are ten venues in South Korea and ten also in Japan. The opening match takes place at the Seoul World Cup Stadium, in Seoul, South Korea, on 31 May, between holders France and Senegal. The Final takes place in the Yokohama International Sports Stadium, in Yokohama, Japan.

South Korea

Nine out of the ten venues in South Korea are within 200 miles (320km) of each other.

1. *Seoul World Cup Stadium, Seoul*
   64,677 capacity

2. *Incheon Munhak Stadium, Incheon*
   52,256 capacity

3. *Suwon World Cup Stadium, Suwon*
   43,138 capacity

4. *Daejeon World Cup Stadium, Daejeon*
   42,407 capacity

5. *Jeonju World Cup Stadium, Jeonju*
   42,477 capacity

6. *Daegu World Cup Stadium, Daegu*
   65,857 capacity

7. *Gwangju World Cup Stadium, Gwangju*
   42,880 capacity

8. *Ulsan Munsu Soccer Stadium, Ulsan*
   43,512 capacity

9. *Busan Sports Complex Main Stadium, Busan*
   55,982 capacity

10. *Jeju World Cup Stadium, Seogwipo, Jeju Island*
    42,256 capacity

Japan

The capital of Japan, Tokyo, has no matches, but Saitama and Yokohama, where the Final will take place, are almost suburbs of Tokyo.

① **Sapporo Dome, Sapporo**
42,122 capacity

② **Miyagi Stadium, Miyagi**
49,133 capacity

③ **Ibaraki Kashima Football Stadium, Kashima**
41,800 capacity

④ **Saitama Soccer Stadium, Urawa**
63,700 capacity

⑤ **Yokohama International Sports Stadium, Yokohama**
70,574 capacity

⑥ **Niigata Stadium, Niigata**
42,700 capacity

⑦ **Shizuoka Stadium Ecopa, Shizuoka**
51,349 capacity

⑧ **Nagai Stadium, Osaka**
50,000 capacity

⑨ **Kobe Universiade Memorial Stadium, Kobe**
42,000 capacity

⑩ **Oita Stadium, Oita**
43,000 capacity

Key to symbols
- group matches
- group matches and round of 16
- group matches and quarter-final
- group matches and 3/4 place play-off
- group matches and semi-final
- group matches and Final

The Stadia

The 2002 World Cup finals are truly unique. Not only are two countries (Japan and Korea), jointly hosting the tournament for the first time, but also there will be a record 20 stadia used for the matches (ten in each country). Incredibly, all of them are practically brand new, built for the competition.

Holders France will play World Cup finals new boys Senegal at the Seoul World Cup Stadium in South Korea's capital city in the opening game

Seoul was the venue for the 1988 Summer Olympic Games, but it was decided to build a new stadium for the 2002 World Cup. The Seoul World Cup Stadium opened late in 2001, and its capacity for the World Cup finals will be almost 65,000, making it the largest football-only stadium in Asia.

The futuristic Sapporo Dome has no fixed pitch. The grass actually grows outside the stadium and is transported inside when there is a football match. Sapporo, like Seoul, has hosted the Olympics, but these were the Winter Games of 1972.

Argentina and England will meet at the Sapporo Dome in what is probably the most eagerly-awaited game of the first round

The Daegu World Cup Stadium may be the third oldest one to be used during the World Cup finals, but it did not open until mid-May 2001

Daegu is the third largest city in South Korea, after Busan and the capital Seoul. As with many of the stadia built for these World Cup finals, the design of the stadium is in keeping with local culture and as well as blending in with its natural surroundings, the shape of the roof is intended to capture the beauty of a traditional Korean house.

The capital of Japan, Tokyo, will not have a single game in the 2002 World Cup, but Yokohama, just 30 minutes by road from the city, will more than make up for it. The Yokohama International Sports Stadium will play host to three first-round group matches, including Japan against Russia, but, more importantly, it will also be the setting for the Final.

The eyes of the world will be on the Yokohama International Sports Stadium on 30 June 2002 when the Final of the World Cup will be played there

Tournament Rules

The tough qualification process has left 32 countries to battle for the title of best in the world. These teams are divided into eight groups of four, with the top two in each group progressing to the second-round knockout stage. From this point, drawn games are not allowed – if a match finishes level at the end of 90 minutes, the following apply:

Extra time: A maximum of 30 minutes in two 15-minute halves – unless a "Golden Goal" is scored.
The "Golden Goal": The first side to score wins as extra-time ends immediately.
Penalties: If there is no goal scored in extra-time, each team has an initial five attempts to settle the contest from the penalty mark. If scores are level after five kicks each, penalties continue until one side comes out on top.

The Golden Boot Award

This glittering award goes to the player who scores the greatest number of goals in the finals. The second and third-highest scorers are awarded Silver and Bronze Boots. England's last winner, with six goals in the Mexico 1986 competition, was Gary Lineker, now a television presenter.

Right: Lineker celebrates one of his World Cup goals
Below: Suker gives Croatia the lead in the 1998 World Cup semi-final against France, but Croatia lost 2-1 in the end, and France won the tournament

The FIFA Fair Play Awards

Since 1993, all players in FIFA tournaments sign "Declarations of Fair Play". The World Cup is the world's biggest sporting event, and despite the pressures of fame and fortune, the top players are expected to set a good example. The awards – trophies and money for youth football – are given to players and teams who have done the most to:

- *play their very best*
- *entertain supporters*
- *avoid arguments with referees*
- *show self-control*
- *be humble in defeat*
- *respect players*
- *set a good example to children*

In 1998, England and France shared the award, having committed least fouls and conducted themselves well. In 2000, Lucas Radebe (Leeds and South Africa) received an award for showing the spirit of "Fair Play" through his conduct on the pitch and his work with underprivileged children off it.

GOLDEN BOOT WINNERS

Year	Player	Country	Goals
1930	Guillermo Stabile	Argentina	8
1934	Oldrich Nejedly	Czechoslovakia	5
1938	Leonidas Da Silva	Brazil	8
1950	Ademir	Brazil	9
1954	Sandor Kocsis	Hungary	11
1958	Just Fontaine	France	13
1962	Vava	Brazil	4
	Garrincha	Brazil	4
	Florian Albert	Hungary	4
	Valentin Ivanov	USSR	4
	Drazan Jerkovic	Yugoslavia	4
	Leonel Sanchez	Chile	4
1966	Eusebio	Portugal	9
1970	Gerd Müller	W Germany	10
1974	Grzegorz Lato	Poland	7
1978	Mario Kempes	Argentina	6
1982	Paolo Rossi	Italy	6
1986	Gary Lineker	England	6
1990	Salvatore Schillaci	Italy	6
1994	Hristo Stoichkov	Bulgaria	6
	Oleg Salenko	Russia	6
1998	Davor Suker	Croatia	6

Meet the Teams

Group A
- France
- Senegal
- Uruguay
- Denmark

Group B
- Spain
- Paraguay
- South Africa
- Slovenia

Group C
- Brazil
- Turkey
- China
- Costa Rica

Group D
- Portugal
- Poland
- USA
- South Korea

Europe provides 15 of the 32 nations at the finals, including the holders France and other former champions England, Germany and Italy, plus newcomers Slovenia.

Three out of the five South American qualifiers have won the World Cup before Argentina, Brazil and Uruguay. It means all the former World Cup winner will be at these finals. Costa Rica won the North/Central American qualifying group.

Group E
- Germany
- Ireland
- Saudi Arabia
- Cameroon

Group F
- Argentina
- England
- Nigeria
- Sweden

Group G
- Italy
- Ecuador
- Croatia
- Mexico

Group H
- Belgium
- Russia
- Tunisia
- Japan

Asia is hosting the World Cup finals for the first time and Africa is most likely to stage the event in 2010. China and Senegal are both newcomers to the World Cup finals. Australia lost a play-off to Uruguay, so no team from Oceania will play in Japan and Korea.

Group A

FRANCE   **SENEGAL**   **URUGUAY**   **DENMARK**

FRANCE, the favourites for Group A, are the reigning European and World Champions. France was a founding nation of the first World Cup in 1930 but only really emerged as a football superpower in the 1980s, making two World Cup semi-finals, and with Olympic and European victories within four years. France have an extremely strong team: Chelsea's Marcel Desailly is one of the best defenders playing and Arsenal's Patrick Vieira can dominate a midfield, while fellow Gunner Thierry Henry (No. 12, above) and Zinedine Zidane (Real Madrid) provide a potent attacking force.

Their opener against **SENEGAL** will be a fascinating contest. The two teams have not met recently but Patrick Vieira was born in Senegal, whilst most of the African team play in the French leagues. Senegal are the only African qualifier never to have played in a World Cup competition before and most of their hopes will rest upon the young shoulders of forward El Hadji Diouf.

URUGUAY

could give France a run for their money. The "Sleeping Giants" of South America are 12th in the all-time World Cup rankings, having won the first tournament in 1930, which they hosted, and again in 1950. Apart from qualifying in 1986 and 1990, they have had little to celebrate since then and much will depend on their Italian league players Pablo Garcia (AC Milan) and Alvaro Recoba (Inter Milan, above).

DENMARK,

who will be competing in their third World Cup, won the European Championship in 1992 and have produced some very fine players, most notably the great goalkeeper Peter Schmeichel. His successor, Thomas Sorensen, is with Sunderland and other leading Danes in the Premiership include Jesper Gronkjaer at Chelsea and Thomas Gravesen at Everton. Denmark's goalscoring hopes rest with Schalke '04 forward Ebbe Sand (No. 11, right), runner-up in the 2000 and 2001 German League Player of The Year Award, who once scored two hat-tricks in just 10 days.

Group B

SPAIN   **PARAGUAY**   **SOUTH AFRICA**   **SLOVENIA**

SPAIN are due for a good World Cup performance having often underachieved in major tournaments, despite producing some of the world's best players in what many now consider the strongest domestic league. Real Madrid, Barcelona and Valencia are dominant in European competition, but the national side has never won the World Cup or even reached the semi-finals, although they finished fourth in 1950. This year's squad has some outstanding players in Raul, Gaizka Mendieta (left) and Juan Valeron, who would all love to emulate Emilio Butragueno, whose tally of four goals against Denmark in 1986 is the second highest for any player in a single World Cup match.

Spain's closest group rival will probably be **PARAGUAY**. Though they have never advanced beyond the second round (1986 and 1998) in their five appearances in the World Cup, they certainly possess the flair and ability to shock teams – after all, they qualified for the 2002 finals before Brazil did. One player to look out for is the colourful goalkeeper Jose Luis Chilavert (far right), who likes to take free-kicks and penalties.

This World Cup will mark 10 years back in the international footballing arena for **SOUTH AFRICA**. They are certainly a team of promise and have qualified for all of the last five African Nations Cups, winning in 1996. They made an early exit in France '98 but went down fighting. Key players include captain Shaun Bartlett, the Charlton Athletic striker, and Lucas Radebe of Leeds United (left).

For a country of just two million inhabitants, which split from Yugoslavia in 1991, **SLOVENIA**'s qualification campaigns for Euro 2000 and now the 2002 World Cup finals were miraculous. Much of Slovenia's success is down to their coach Srecko "Lucky" Katanec, a world-class player in his time and now a national hero. On the field, the star player is striker Zlatko Zahovic.

Group C

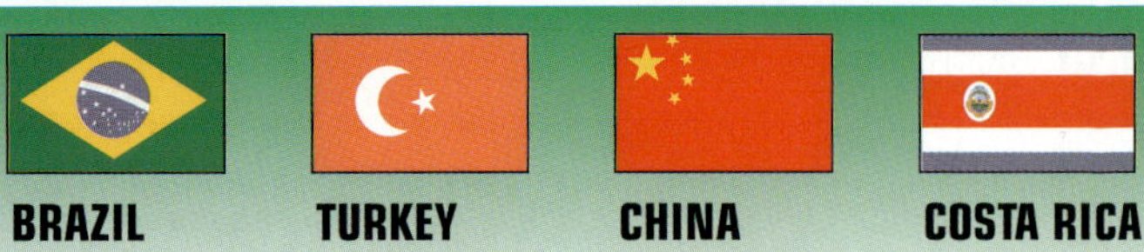

BRAZIL **TURKEY** **CHINA** **COSTA RICA**

Four-time World Cup Champions (most recently in 1994) and beaten finalists in 1950 and 1998, **BRAZIL** boast the best record in world football. Most people would also rate the former Brazilian striker Pelé as the greatest player of all time. His 1281 goals in 1363 professional matches will surely never be beaten. He played in each of the renowned Brazilian teams that won World Cups in 1958, 1962 and 1970. Today's star players are Rivaldo, Ronaldo and Roberto Carlos (in blue, left), the full-back with a thundering shot.

However, the unthinkable nearly happened when Brazil almost failed to qualify for Korea/Japan 2002. Of their 18 group matches, they managed only nine victories and three draws, finishing third.

TURKEY haven't reached the World Cup finals since 1954. They surprised everyone by making it to the quarter-finals stage of Euro 2000 after crashing out of Euro '96 without scoring. By far their most influential player is Inter Milan striker Hakan Sukur (top), who was Europe's top goalscorer in 1996/97.

CHINA are competing in their first ever World Cup finals after five victories and one draw in their first six Asian group games. Their star player and captain is Fan Zhiyi (No. 5, left), formerly of Crystal Palace and now with Dundee.

COSTA RICA will be looking to repeat the performance of their first ever World Cup in 1990, when they reached the last 16 with surprise victories over Sweden and Scotland. Paulo Wanchope (heading ball, below) of Manchester City leads the attack while Hernan Medford, the country's most famous player, will be 34 when the competition commences but will be just as crucial to the side as he was 12 years ago.

Group D

PORTUGAL　　**POLAND**　　**USA**　　**SOUTH KOREA**

Sometimes described as the "European Brazilians", due to the exciting football they can play, **PORTUGAL** have players in this World Cup who would be described as world class in any era, especially Luis Figo (Real Madrid) and Rui Costa (AC Milan, left). Moreover, many of the national team are players who featured in the FIFA Youth World Cup winning sides in 1989 and 1991 and who now possess the top-level experience to provide a real threat to any team. The country's best performance to date was in 1966 when they came third, led by legendary striker and Golden Boot winner Eusebio.

POLAND have enjoyed a resurgence of the World Cup form that took them to the semi-finals in 1974 and 1982, thanks largely to Nigerian-born striker Emmanuel Olisadebe

(celebrating, right). His change to Polish citizenship was crucial in taking his adopted country to this World Cup. Poland qualified for Korea/Japan 2002 undefeated in seven consecutive games and will be hard on the heels of Portugal. The squad also includes Liverpool goalkeeper Jerzy Dudek who, since moving from Feyenoord in Holland, has impressed many.

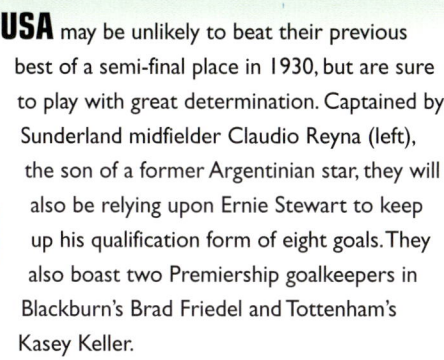

USA may be unlikely to beat their previous best of a semi-final place in 1930, but are sure to play with great determination. Captained by Sunderland midfielder Claudio Reyna (left), the son of a former Argentinian star, they will also be relying upon Ernie Stewart to keep up his qualification form of eight goals. They also boast two Premiership goalkeepers in Blackburn's Brad Friedel and Tottenham's Kasey Keller.

Co-hosts **SOUTH KOREA** are still seeking their first ever victory in five World Cup appearances and will be hoping to surpass the 1966 quarter-final appearance of their rivals North Korea. They have a top quality striker in Seol Ki Hyeon (No. 11, below), who plays for Belgian team Anderlecht and much will depend upon him.

Group E

GERMANY

IRELAND

SAUDI ARABIA

CAMEROON

GERMANY have won both the World Cup and the European Championship three times each and are the second most successful World Cup nation, though they are currently seen by many as a side in transition. Despite being crushed in qualification by England (5–1) and drawing twice with Finland, Rudi Voeller's side made it through with a play-off victory over Ukraine. Two of Germany's leading players are Hertha Berlin striker Sebastian Deisler and Bayer Leverkusen midfielder Michael Ballack. Also, Bayern Munich goalkeeper Oliver Kahn (above) is rated among the world's best.

Under Jack Charlton, one of England's 1966 World Cup victors, the **REPUBLIC OF IRELAND** enjoyed their best run, qualifying for two World Cups (1990 and 1994) and the European Championship in 1988. It was a hard act to follow when Mick McCarthy took over in 1996 and Ireland experienced dreadful luck in being knocked-out in the play-offs for France '98 and Euro 2000. The dramatic qualification for this World Cup included a shock defeat of Holland – shouldering that side full of stars into third place and, to general disbelief, out of the World Cup – and a nail-biting play-off victory over Iran. Led and inspired by Manchester United captain Roy Keane, Ireland will look to his namesake Robbie (right), of Leeds, for goals.

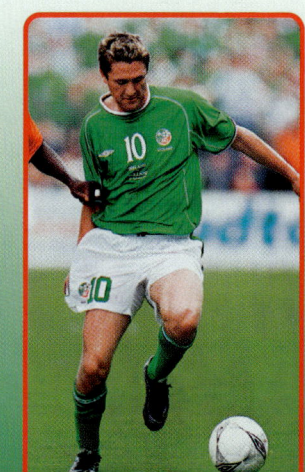

This will be **SAUDI ARABIA**'s third successive World Cup, but it will be an heroic achievement to match the exploits of the 1994 team, which made it through to the second round. Striker Sami Al-Jaber (left), who had a brief spell at Nationwide League Wolverhampton Wanderers in 2000, will be their key player.

CAMEROON – "The Indomitable Lions" – are the only team from the African continent ever to reach the quarter-finals of a World Cup (1990). Their player of the moment is striker Patrick Mboma, who has prompted comparisons to the country's legendary striker Roger Milla, whose four tournament goals as a 38-year-old put Cameroon on the map in Italia '90. Another player to look out for is Arsenal's Lauren (right), who won Olympic gold with Cameroon in 2000.

Group F

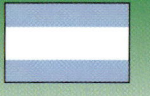

ARGENTINA **ENGLAND** **NIGERIA** **SWEDEN**

With their all-star line-up, **ARGENTINA** are favourites to lead the "Group of Death" and win the World Cup. Argentina won the World Cup at home in 1978 and again in Mexico in 1986. The strongest of the current South American teams features an incomparable midfield and forward line of Hernan Crespo (Lazio, scoring against Paraguay, left), Juan Sebastian Veron (Manchester United), Kily Gonzalez (Valencia), Gabriel Batistuta (Roma), Javier Zanetti (Inter Milan) and Ariel Ortega (River Plate). The most famous Argentinian player of all time is Diego Maradona, a footballing genius whose two goals against England in Mexico '86 (one a brilliant solo run, the other a handball) ended their dreams in the quarter-finals.

Though **ENGLAND** founded modern football, it was not until 1950 that the country entered the World Cup. With their triumph over West Germany in the 1966 final, Bobby Moore's heroes made that year the most famous in English footballing history. Apart from that victory, England reached the semi-finals only one more time, losing to West Germany on penalties in 1990. But with David Beckham as skipper and Michael Owen and Paul Scholes (right) scoring goals along the way, England avenged that defeat in the qualifying stages and go to Japan full of hope.

This will be the third World Cup for **NIGERIA**'s "Super Eagles", who have progressed to the second round on both of their previous attempts. They certainly have a talented squad to choose from, which includes Arsenal's striker Nwankwo Kanu (No. 4, left), Chelsea defender Celestine Babayaro and PSG's Augustine "Jay Jay" Okocha.

A 5–2 defeat by Brazil in the 1958 final represents **SWEDEN**'s best finish to date and the late 1990s were particularly disappointing, with qualification failures for Euro '96 and France '98. However, they have an excellent unbeaten record against England stretching back to 1968. Most of the current squad play outside Sweden, with two of the biggest names being Henrik Larsson (right), the outstanding Celtic striker, and Arsenal's Freddie Ljungberg.

Group G

ITALY **ECUADOR** **CROATIA** **MEXICO**

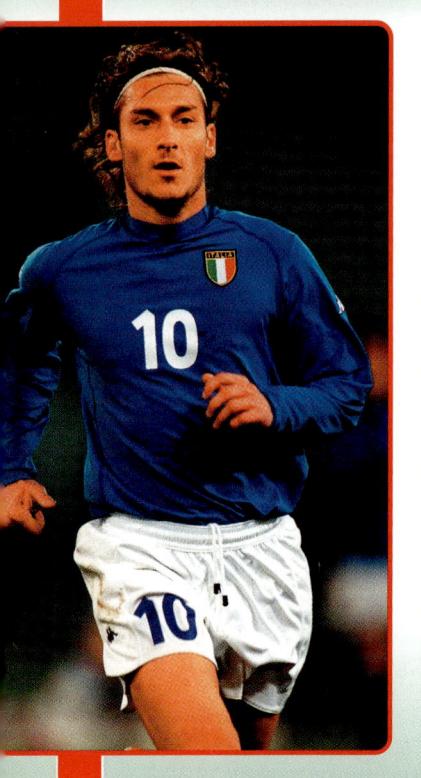

World Cup competitions never fail to bring the very best out of **ITALY** and they possess the third-finest record, lifting the trophy three times and losing two finals. However, they have not won the competition since their defeat of West Germany in 1982 and the national team perhaps suffers from the presence of so many top quality players from other countries in Serie A. They will nevertheless be strong favourites to win this group, with a formidable team featuring Roma's Francesco Totti (left), Juventus striker Alessandro Del Piero and captain Paolo Maldini, the AC Milan defender and Italy's most-capped player.

ECUADOR are an unknown quantity at international level since this is their first World Cup, but they caught the eye in qualifying with a surprise victory over Brazil. With established players such as Southampton striker Agustin "Tin Tin" Delgado (right), and brilliant new players such as Walter Ayovi in the team, Ecuador are an exciting prospect.

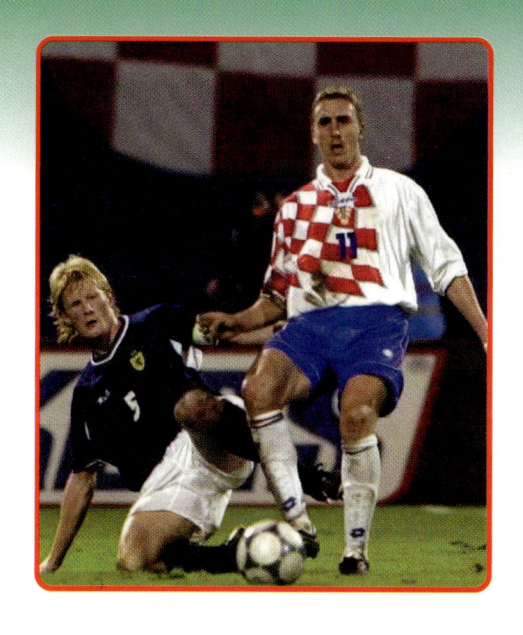

CROATIA's national team was founded only 11 years ago and this will be their second World Cup finals. They surprisingly reached the semi-finals in 1998 (going one better than their quarter-final appearance at Euro '96), eventually falling to France. They qualified for these finals without losing a single match. Their strong squad this year includes players in top German, Italian and English leagues, including strikers Alen Boksic (above) of Middlesbrough and Davor Suker, the Golden Boot winner in 1998.

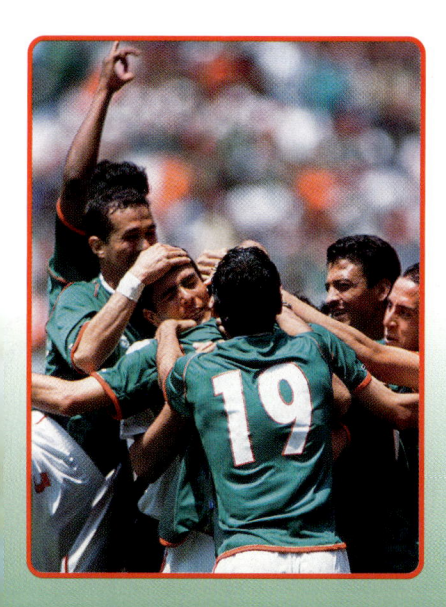

MEXICO have qualified for their 12th World Cup finals and will be striving to go beyond the quarter-finals, which they reached in 1986 when their current manager, Javier Aguirre, played. They are a team of tough tacklers and possess excellent ball skills, none more so than Cuauhtemoc Blanco (being mobbed by delighted team-mates, above), a powerful forward with fantastic shooting abilities and trickery on the ball. He was crucial to Mexico's qualifying campaign, and scored nine goals in four matches.

Group H

BELGIUM **RUSSIA** **TUNISIA** **JAPAN**

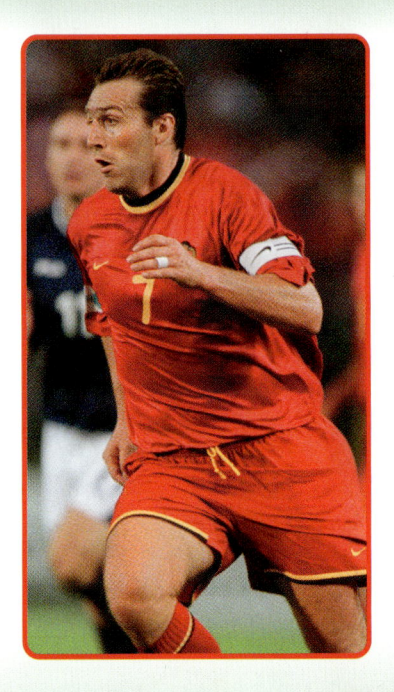

BELGIUM have always been a steady but unspectacular World Cup team, and on qualifying for this tournament became the only qualifier to have reached the finals through the qualifying process six times in a row. They will probably be the favourites for this relatively weak group. Belgium did not lose a game in France '98, but nor did they win and their three draws were not enough to take them any further in the tournament. Captain Marc Wilmots (left), of Schalke '04 in the top German league, will be hoping to lead his team to better things this time.

RUSSIA's best World Cup performance, as semi-finalists, came in 1966 in England when they were part of the Soviet Union. The current squad, with a reputation for hard tackling, is a mixture of young and experienced players. One to look out for is striker Vladimir Beschastnykh of Spartak Moscow, whose hat-trick against Switzerland in 2001 destroyed the Swiss side's qualification hopes.

TUNISIA became the first African team to win a game on football's greatest stage when they defeated Mexico 3–1 in 1978 and this will be their third World Cup. Their key striker is Adel Sellimi (left), who plays for Freiburg in the German Bundesliga, but he will need strong support if they are to progress beyond the first round.

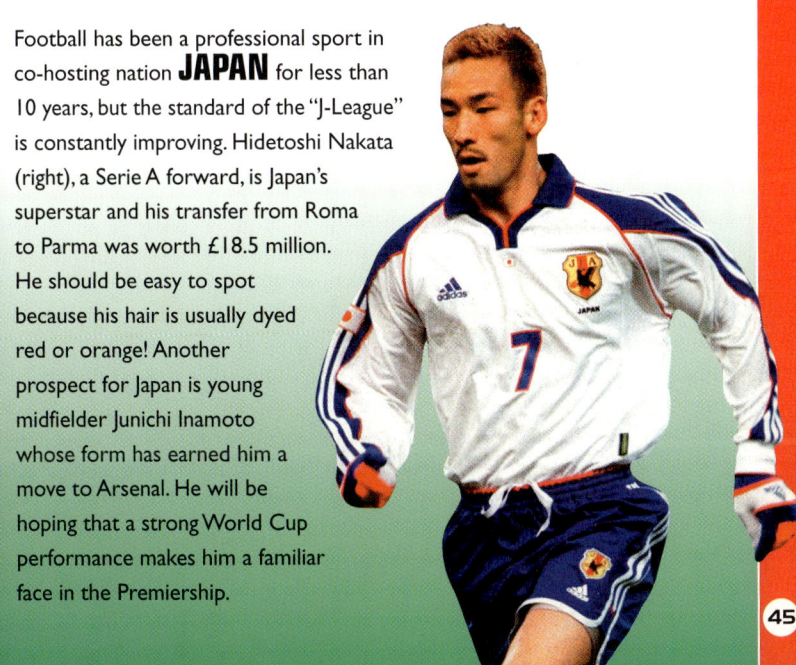

Football has been a professional sport in co-hosting nation **JAPAN** for less than 10 years, but the standard of the "J-League" is constantly improving. Hidetoshi Nakata (right), a Serie A forward, is Japan's superstar and his transfer from Roma to Parma was worth £18.5 million. He should be easy to spot because his hair is usually dyed red or orange! Another prospect for Japan is young midfielder Junichi Inamoto whose form has earned him a move to Arsenal. He will be hoping that a strong World Cup performance makes him a familiar face in the Premiership.

World Superstars

Zinedine Zidane, France

Date of Birth: 23.06.1972 • **Club:** Real Madrid • **Position:** Midfielder

Zinedine Zidane was regarded as one of the world's best players long before he headed two of France's goals in their 3–0 victory over Brazil to win the 1998 World Cup Final.

The Frenchman, nicknamed Zizou, also helped his country win the European Championship in 2000, and has himself won both European and World Player of the Year awards.

Born in Marseille of Algerian parents, he started his career at local club Cannes before moving to Bordeaux in 1992. After a starring role in their European campaign and then for France at Euro '96, he moved on to Italian giants Juventus. But his biggest move came last year when he joined Real Madrid for a world record £45.6 million.

For a big man, Zidane has delicate ball control, a superb range of passing and a goalscoring instinct that makes him one of the greatest attacking midfielders in the modern game. With him at the heart of the side, it is no wonder France are among the favourites to win in the Far East and remain world champions.

Rivaldo, Brazil

Date of Birth: 19.04.1972 • **Club:** Barcelona • **Position:** Midfielder

Brazil's attacking midfielder Rivaldo is regarded as one of the best footballers in the world and was voted World Player of the Year in 1999.

Rivaldo's career started back in Brazil, where he played for leading clubs Palmeiras and Corinthians among others. After starring for Brazil in the 1996 Olympic Games, he made the move to play in Europe. At Spain's Deportivo La Coruna he scored 21 goals in 41 matches, a remarkable record from midfield, and was snapped up by Barcelona a year later for a then record £16 million to replace his fellow Brazilian Ronaldo.

A heavily superstitious man, Rivaldo's first step on to any football pitch is always with his right foot, as he believes this brings him luck. But it is with his left foot that he weaves most magic, whether it is hitting powerful swerving shots on goal or sending long-range passes of pinpoint accuracy. That's not to forget how he runs past players with outstanding close control.

Astonishingly Rivaldo was dropped during Brazil's struggle to qualify for Japan and Korea, and he's not always considered the best of team players, but on his day there is no doubt that he can be a match-winner.

Raul, Spain

Date of Birth: 27.06.1977 • **Club:** Real Madrid • **Position:** Striker

For someone who will not be 25 until the latter stage of this year's tournament, Raul has already achieved more than most players can even dream of.

The Spanish striker has helped Real Madrid win a handful of domestic cup and league titles, the European Cup twice (in 1998 and 2000) and he has also appeared for his country at the 1996 Olympic Games, the 1998 World Cup in France and at Euro 2000.

Raul started his career in the Atletico Madrid youth ranks, but when that system was controversially disbanded, he joined rivals Real Madrid. He became the youngest player to represent the famous old club when he made his debut at the age of 17 years and four months, and his goals helped them win the league title in his first season.

He is not the biggest of forwards, but is quick and alert and that has enabled him to play as either an out-and-out striker or in a more withdrawn role, setting-up chances for his team-mates as well as scoring freely himself. If Spain are to improve on their dismal World Cup record, Raul will be central to their chances.

Luis Figo, Portugal

Date of Birth: 04.11.1972 • **Club:** Real Madrid • **Position:** Midfielder/ Striker

Luis Figo is officially the finest footballer on the planet, having been voted World Footballer of the Year in 2001, a year after winning the European Footballer of the Year title.

The Pride of Portugal is equally popular in Spain, where he was voted player of the season for four consecutive years by Spanish fans. Figo started his career at Sporting Lisbon before moving to Barcelona in 1996, where he became a superstar.

By then he had already helped Portugal to great success at youth and under-21 levels, before winning his first full cap. He was central to Portugal's success at Euro 2000, where they reached the semi-finals. Soon afterwards he was transferred controversially to Barcelona's bitter rivals Real Madrid for a world record £42 million.

Primarily a wide player, Figo can play also through the centre of midfield and possesses a powerful shot, as well as being a great crosser of the ball. With Figo leading Portugal again, they are sure to be among the favourites this time.

Roy Keane, Republic of Ireland

Date of Birth: 10.08.1971 • **Club:** Manchester United • **Position:** Midfielder

The Manchester United and Republic of Ireland skipper is one of the most inspirational players in the world, and has been described by his club manager Sir Alex Ferguson as the complete footballer.

Keane is a genuine all-rounder, who can score goals with either feet or head, set up chances for his team-mates and tackle like a tiger – indeed he is equally comfortable in defence as he is in his more regular midfield role.

He is one of the hardest tacklers and most competitive players in world football, so it is not surprising that he was considered a great boxing prospect before he became a professional footballer.

Brian Clough spotted him playing for tiny Cobh Ramblers in the south of Ireland and signed him for Nottingham Forest for just £25,000 in 1990. Ferguson took him to United three years later for £3.75 million, a record between British clubs at the time, and Keane has been at the forefront of the club's rise to dominance in England and Europe.

Although he missed out when United won the Champions League in 1999, Keane was voted Footballer of the Year by both the players and the Football Writers Association the following season and is now hoping for the same sort of success with his national side.

Juan Sebastian Veron,
Argentina

Date of Birth: 09.03.1975 • **Club:** Manchester United • **Position:** Midfielder

Juan Sebastian Veron became the most expensive player in Britain when Manchester United signed him from Lazio in the summer of 2001 for £28m. But the tall midfielder was already well-known by English fans for his abilities at international level as part of the Argentina team that knocked England out of the World Cup in France '98.

Veron's father, also called Juan, was a leading international back in the 1960s, and his son followed the same path, joining Estudiantes as a youngster before going to the great Boca Juniors.

Soon he was on his way to Europe, first with Sampdoria in Italy's Serie A and then on to Parma and Lazio, where he played under Sven-Göran Eriksson, who is now England manager. Veron was instrumental as Lazio won the Italian league and cup double as well as the European Cup–Winners' Cup in 1999.

A great passer of the ball, with a fierce shot and amazing stamina, Veron is one of the world's best midfielders and a major reason why Argentina are among the hot favourites to win the World Cup again.

Players to Watch out for

Alvaro Recoba, Uruguay
Date of Birth: 17.03.1976 • **Club:** Inter Milan • **Position:** Striker

Alvaro Recoba is earning his place alongside the greatest Uruguayan strikers. He made his professional debut at 17 for Danubio and then moved to Nacional, and in his first five seasons in Uruguay amassed 62 goals in 58 appearances. In 1997 he was signed by Inter and has now established himself as a consistent performer for them and as one of the most feared strikers in Serie A.

Emmanuel Olisadebe, Poland
Date of Birth: 22.12.1978 • **Club:** Panathinaikos • **Position:** Striker

Olisadebe might never have played for Poland had his homeland Nigeria selected him for their national team. He was disappointed to be overlooked for the Nigerian side and in 2000, while playing for Polonia Warsaw in the Polish league, obtained Polish citizenship with the help of the nation's footballing legend Zbigniew Boniek. Nigeria perhaps regretted their loss when Olisadebe scored seven goals in Poland's 10 qualification matches.

Michael Ballack, Germany
Date of Birth: 26.09.1976 • **Club:** Bayer Leverkusen • **Position:** Midfielder

Ballack started his career with Kaiserslautern in 1997 before transferring two seasons later to Bayer Leverkusen. An attacking midfielder and exceptional passer, he was initially slow to make an impact with Bayer due to a knee injury. However, he has now established himself as a leading midfielder in Germany and will hope to fulfil his considerable talent on the world stage.

Patrick Mboma, Cameroon

Date of Birth: 15.11.1970 • **Club:** Parma • **Position:** Striker

A mathematics graduate, Mboma's first season was for Paris St Germain (1993). He struggled and was loaned to third division Chateauroux, scoring 17 goals in 29 games before being recalled to Paris. In 1997 he was outstanding for Osaka in the J-League with 25 goals in 28 matches, scoring the fastest goal (26 seconds) and the league's first hat-trick. In 1998 he transferred to Cagliari and then Parma.

Hidetoshi Nakata, Japan

Date of Birth: 22.01.1977 • **Club:** Parma • **Position:** Midfielder

At 21, "Hide" became the youngest ever Asian Footballer of the Year. The talents he displayed in France '98 made him a target for newly-promoted Italian club Perugia. After two years there he moved to Roma for a season and then to his current club Parma in 2001. This colourful character will undoubtedly be an inspiration for many young footballers when he returns to play on home territory in the World Cup.

Robbie Keane, Republic of Ireland

Date of Birth: 08.07.1980 • **Club:** Leeds United • **Position:** Striker

Keane's career started in 1996 with Wolves and after 24 goals in 67 starts, he moved to Coventry, scoring twice on his 1999 debut. Inter Milan signed him for what turned out to be a disappointing season for them, giving the Irishman little opportunity to shine. But he returned to England and Leeds United, who paid £11m, and was an instant hit with his livewire displays. Look out for his trademark handspring goal celebration.

World Cup Trivia

DID YOU KNOW?

● **The British home nations** – England, Scotland, Wales and Northern Ireland – have qualified for the same finals tournament only once, in 1958. None progressed beyond the quarter-finals.

The successful Italian team after the 1938 World Cup Final when they became the first country to win the World Cup twice in a row; their coach on both occasions, Vittorio Pozzo, is showing off the Jules Rimet Trophy

● **The youngest goalscorer** in World Cup history, at 17 years and 239 days, was Pelé of Brazil, when he scored against Wales in Sweden 1958.

● **The only player to** score four goals in a World Cup game and still end up on the losing side was Ernst Willimowski of Poland in 1938, as his team lost 6–5 to Brazil, for whom Leonidas also scored four.

● **Oleg Salenko of Russia** is the only player to have scored five goals in one match in the finals, against Cameroon in 1994.

● **The biggest victory** in the final stages was in 1982 when Hungary destroyed El Salvador 10–1, in Spain.

● **The biggest victory** in the qualification stages came in 2001 when Australia beat American Samoa by a staggering 31 goals to nil!

Geoff Hurst's controversial second goal in the 1966 Final is still the subject of debate because no picture taken from the goal-line has ever come to light

● **The most goals in** a single match in the finals is 12, which came when Austria beat host nation Switzerland 7–5 in 1954.

● **Germany's Lothar Matthäus** is the most experienced World Cup player with 25 appearances in the final stages between 1982 and 1998. He, and Mexico's Antonio Carbajal, are the only men to have played in five finals.

● **Brazil are the** only team to have appeared in all 16 finals tournaments.

● **The youngest player** ever to have appeared in a World Cup finals match, at 17 years and 41 days, was Norman Whiteside of Northern Ireland at the 1982 tournament in Spain.

● **The most successful** team at winning penalty shoot-outs is West Germany. They have been involved in three shoot-outs and have won all of them, missing only one penalty in 14 attempts.

● **The current World** Cup trophy is the second to be used. The original Jules Rimet trophy, named after the tournament's founder, was presented permanently to Brazil in 1970 when they won it for the third time.

ALL-TIME WORLD CUP GOALSCORERS 1930-1998

Gerd Müller (GER) 14
Just Fontaine (FRA) 13
Pelé (BRA) 12
Sandor Kocsis (HUN) 11
Jürgen Klinsmann (GER) 11
Helmut Kahn (GER) 10
Teofilio Cubillas (PERU) 10
Gary Lineker (ENG) 10
Grzegorz Lato (POL) 10
Gabriel Batistuta (ARG) 9
Roberto Baggio (ITA) 9
Paolo Rossi (ITA) 9
Uwe Seeler (GER) 9
Jairzinho (BRA) 9
Eusebio (POR) 9
Karl-Heinz Rummenigge (GER) 9
Vava (BRA) 9
Ademir (BRA) 9

World Cup Quiz Answers on page 58

1 When and where was the first World Cup played?

2 What was the original World Cup trophy called?

3 Which nation has won the World Cup most times – and how many?

4 Which player has the record for the number of goals scored in a tournament?

5 In which year did England win the World Cup and whom did they beat in the final?

6 Which Italian club did Sven-Göran Eriksson manage before taking over as England coach?

7 Against which country did David Beckham score a last-minute free-kick in England's final qualifying game last October?

8 In which year did England last defeat Sweden?

9 Who is the only player to have scored a hat-trick in a World Cup final?

10 Who was the last Englishman to win the Golden Boot Award?

11 Which international footballer has the nickname "Zizou"?

12 Who scored twice in the 1958 World Cup Final and once in the 1970 World Cup Final?

13 Which team is nicknamed "The Super Eagles"?

14 Which famous Argentinian player scored a goal against England in the 1986 World Cup quarter-final with his hand?

15 Who is the reigning World Footballer of the Year?

16 Who was the French goalkeeper in the 1998 World Cup winning side?

17 Who was the captain of England in the 1966 World Cup?

18 Name one of the English Premiership clubs Davor Suker played for.

19 Which English Premiership club does Agustin Delgado of Ecuador play for?

20 Who is the current European Footballer of the Year?

21 Which Dutch side did Poland goalkeeper Jerzy Dudek play for before joining Liverpool?

22 Who was the England manager during the 1998 World Cup and which club does he currently manage?

23 Who was the leading scorer in the 1998 World Cup finals?

24 What animal is featured on the England badge?

25 Name one Nigerian international playing in the English Premiership.

World Cup Quiz Answers

1) The first World Cup took place in 1930 in Uruguay.
2) The Jules Rimet trophy, after the FIFA president who founded the tournament.
3) Brazil, four times.
4) Just Fontaine (above) of France scored 13 goals in 1958.
5) 1966, when England beat West Germany 4–2 in the final.
6) Lazio.
7) Greece.
8) 1968.
9) Geoff Hurst, for England in 1966.
10) Gary Lineker, in 1986.
11) Zinedine Zidane.
12) Pelé of Brazil.
13) Nigeria.
14) Diego Maradona.
15) Luis Figo of Portugal.
16) Fabien Barthez.
17) Bobby Moore.
18) Arsenal or West Ham.
19) Southampton.
20) Michael Owen.
21) Feyenoord.
22) Glenn Hoddle, currently the manager of Tottenham Hotspur.
23) Davor Suker of Croatia with six goals.
24) The lion.
25) Celestine Babayaro or Nwankwo Kanu.

Crossword solution

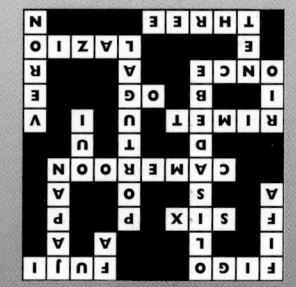

World Cup Crossword

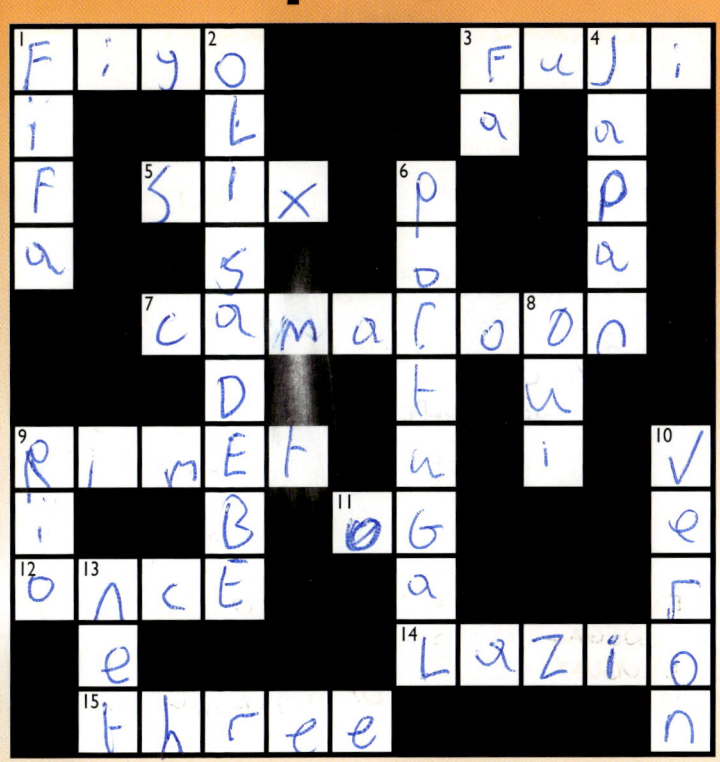

	F	i	y	O			F	u	j	i
	i		L				a		a	
	F		S	i	x		p		p	
	a		S				D		a	
		c	a	m	a	r	o	o	n	
			D				t			
	R	i	n	E			u	i		V
	i		B			O	G			e
	O	n	c	E		a				r
	e					L	a	Z	i	O
	t	h	r	e	e					n

ACROSS

1. Beat David Beckham to be voted 2001 World Footballer of the Year (4)
3. The highest mountain in 4 Down (4)
5. Number of goals Gary Lineker scored to win the 1986 Golden Boot Award (3)
7. The 'Indomitable Lions' of Africa, for whom Roger Milla used to play (8)
9. The original World Cup was called 'The Jules _____ Trophy' (5)
11. Initials a player does not want to see on the scoresheet, indicating scoring at the wrong end (2)
12. The number of times England has won the World Cup (4)
14. Italian club which Sven-Göran Eriksson managed before moving to England (5)
15. Number of times Italy have won the World Cup and the number of goals in a hat-trick (5)

DOWN

1. Initials of the governing body of World Football (4)
2. Surname of Poland's star striker, originally from Nigeria (9)
3. Initials of the governing body of English football (2)
4. Tokyo is the capital of this hosting country (5)
6. Number 1 Across and Rui Costa play for this European country (8)
8. Can France lift the World Cup again? They say yes! (3)
9. Spanish for 'river' and the Christian name of Leeds United's star defender (3)
10. Surname of Manchester United's South American star midfielder (5)
13. Fisherman's tool, also useful for stopping a ball (3)

World Cup Finals Progress Chart

Keep a running record of the 2002 World Cup finals with your own World Cup Finals Progress Chart. When the first round is completed you can fill in the tables for the eight groups, below, then plan for the second round and the rest of the knockout stages on the following two pages. Fill in the group winners and the runners-up for Round Two, with the scores, then see which countries will be meeting each other in the quarter-finals and semi-finals. You may not be able to go to the Final in Yokohama at the end of June, but you will have a permanent record and this is the next best thing.

FIRST ROUND

GROUP A – Final Table
France Senegal Uruguay Denmark

#	Team	P	W	D	L	F	A	Pts
1	DENMARK	3	2	1	0	5	2	7
2	SENEGAL	3	1	2	0	5	4	5
3	URUGUAY	3	0	2	1	4	5	2
4	FRANCE	3	0	1	2	0	3	1

GROUP B – Final Table
Spain Paraguay South Africa Slovenia

#	Team	P	W	D	L	F	A	Pts
1	SPAIN	3	3	0	0	9	4	9
2	PARAGUAY	3	1	1	1	6	6	4
3	S. AFRICA	3	1	1	1	5	5	4
4	SLOVENIA	3	0	0	3	2	7	0

GROUP C – Final Table
Brazil Turkey China Costa Rica

#	Team	P	W	D	L	F	A	Pts
1	BRAZIL	3	3	0	0	11	3	9
2	TURKEY	3	1	1	1	5	3	4
3	COSTA RICA	3	1	1	1	5	6	4
4	CHINA	3	0	0	3	0	9	0

GROUP D – Final Table
Portugal Poland USA South Korea

Team	P	W	D	L	F	A	Pts
1 S. KOREA	3	2	1	0	4	1	7
2 U.S.A.	3	1	1	1	5	6	4
3 PORTUGAL	3	1	0	2	6	4	3
4 POLAND	3	1	0	2	3	7	3

GROUP E – Final Table
Germany Ireland Saudi Arabia Cameroon

Team	P	W	D	L	F	A	Pts
1 GERMANY	3	2	1	0	11	1	7
2 IRELAND	3	1	2	0	5	2	5
3 CAMEROON	3	1	1	1	2	3	4
4 SAUDI ARABIA	3	0	0	3	0	12	0

GROUP F – Final Table
Argentina England Nigeria Sweden

Team	P	W	D	L	F	A	Pts
1 SWEDEN	3	1	2	0	4	3	5
2 ENGLAND	3	1	2	0	2	1	5
3 ARGENTINA	3	1	1	1	2	2	4
4 NIGERIA	3	0	1	2	1	3	1

GROUP G – Final Table
Italy Ecuador Croatia Mexico

Team	P	W	D	L	F	A	Pts
1 MEXICO	3	2	1	0	4	2	7
2 ITALY	3	1	1	1	4	3	4
3 CROATIA	3	1	0	2	2	3	3
4 ECUADOR	3	1	0	2	2	4	3

GROUP H – Final Table
Belgium Russia Tunisia Japan

Team	P	W	D	L	F	A	Pts
1 JAPAN	3	2	1	0	5	2	7
2 BELGIUM	3	1	2	0	6	5	5
3 RUSSIA	3	1	0	2	4	4	3
4 TUNISIA	3	0	1	2	1	5	1

SECOND ROUND

GAME 1 – June 15: Seogwipo

[1] GERMANY v PARAGUAY **[0]**
Winner of Group E — Runner-up Group B

GAME 2 – June 15: Niigata

[0] DENMARK v ENGLAND **[3]**
Winner of Group A — Runner-up Group F

GAME 3 – June 16: Oita

[1] SWEDEN v SENEGAL **[2]**
Winner of Group F — Runner-up Group A
SENEGAL GOLDEN GOAL

GAME 4 – June 16: Suwon

[1] SPAIN v IRELAND **[1]**
Winner of Group B — Runner-up Group E
SPAIN 3-2 PENALTIES

GAME 5 – June 17: Jeonju

[0] MEXICO v U.S.A **[2]**
Winner of Group G — Runner-up Group D

GAME 6 – June 17: Kobe

[2] BRAZIL v BELGIUM **[0]**
Winner of Group C — Runner-up Group H

GAME 7 – June 18: Miyagi

[0] JAPAN v TURKEY **[1]**
Winner of Group H — Runner-up Group C

GAME 8 – June 18: Daejeon

[2] S. KOREA v ITALY **[1]**
Winner of Group D — Runner-up Group G
GOLDEN GOAL